M. Houghton Whitcomb

Souvenir Cook Book

Tried and approved recipes

M. Houghton Whitcomb

Souvenir Cook Book
Tried and approved recipes

ISBN/EAN: 9783744791809

Printed in Europe, USA, Canada, Australia, Japan

Cover: Foto ©Lupo / pixelio.de

More available books at **www.hansebooks.com**

"SOUVENIR"

COOK BOOK

• -•- •

TRIED AND APPROVED RECIPES

COMPILED BY

M. HOUGHTON WHITCOMB

" It is the bounty of nature that we live, but of philosophy that we live well "

Beacon Press
Thomas Todd, 1 Somerset Street, Boston
1892

SALUTATORY.

. *As this book needs neither apology nor self-praise and deserves not self-depreciation — does not seek to compliment — it therefore has no preface to write. It only desires to say, by way of explanation, that every recipe in it is the result of actual and approved trial.*

THIS BOOK is dedicated to those noble wives and mothers who, by earnest striving, seek to make of home a haven of rest and comfort, where all can dwell together in sweet peace and — CONCORD.   M. H. W.

❊ BREAD, BISCUIT, ETC. ❊

Experience does take dreadfully high school wages,
But he teaches like no other. — *Carlyle.*

YEAST.

Boil and mash six large potatoes; pour over them six quarts boiling water and strain; add cup salt, one cup sugar; let it stand until nearly cool, then add one cup yeast (or one yeast cake); leave in a warm place, and let it stand until fermented. This yeast never sours.

BROWN BREAD.

One pint sour milk, one cup rye meal, one cup Indian meal, one cup graham, one cup flour, one cup molasses, pinch of salt, one teaspoonful soda, a few raisins. Steam four hours, then brown in the oven.

BROWN BREAD.

Two cups rye meal, two of Indian meal, one cup flour, one cup molasses, three and one half cups sour milk, one teaspoonful soda. Bake four hours very slowly.

CORN CAKE.

One egg, one half cup sugar, one cup sour milk, one half cup Indian meal, one cup flour, one teaspoonful soda, a pinch of salt.

BISCUIT.

One cup milk, a small piece of butter, two and a half teaspoonfuls (not heaping) of baking powder, and two cupfuls of flour.

WHITE BREAD.

Two quarts flour, tablespoonful of lard, one quart of warm milk, one large spoonful sugar, one half teaspoonful salt, one half cup yeast; let it rise over night, knead in the morning, rise again in the tins. Bake an hour in a moderate oven.

PARKER HOUSE ROLLS.

One quart of flour, half tablespoonful butter, half tablespoonful lard, one third cup sugar, one pint milk cooled, a little salt, one half cup yeast; set to rise in a warm place; when light, stir down and rise again; when well risen, knead and roll out half an inch, spread on a little butter, cut oblong, double over in form of half circle, let rise again, then bake.

MRS. L'S ROLLS.

One pint and a half sweet milk boiled; while still warm, put in butter the size of an egg, three tablespoonfuls of sugar, a little salt, one half cake of compressed yeast; when light, mould fifteen minutes; let rise again, cut into round cakes, spread each half with butter, and fold over the other half. Put into pans; when light, bake in a quick oven.

GRAHAM BREAD.

One quart of warm water, one half cup molasses, one half cup sugar, four cups graham, four cups flour, a little salt, one yeast cake; rise over night; let bake one hour.

GRAHAM ROLLS No. 1.

Two cups sour milk, one half cup molasses, one fourth cup sugar, two tablespoonfuls melted lard, one teaspoonful soda, graham flour enough for a stiff batter. Bake in gem pans.

GRAHAM ROLLS No. 2.

Two cups graham meal, one half cup flour, one egg, one half cup sugar, a little salt, one teaspoonful soda, two of cream tartar, butter size of a walnut.

RYE CAKES.

One pint hot milk, one cup rye meal, two cups flour, one half cup sugar ; cool, then add one half cup of yeast. Let this rise over night ; in the morning add one half teaspoonful saleratus and two eggs.

RYE MUFFINS.

One pint rye, one pint flour, one half cup yeast, one half cup molasses, pinch of salt, one teaspoonful soda.

SQUASH MUFFINS.

One cup squash, one egg, one half cup sugar, one cup milk, one teaspoonful cream tartar, one half teaspoonful soda, flour enough to stiffen.

CORN CAKE No. 1.

One cup sour milk, one cup flour, one cup Indian meal, one half cup sugar, butter size of an egg, one teaspoonful soda.

CORN CAKE No. 2.

One cup sweet milk, one cup flour, one cup Indian meal, one half cup sugar, one egg, one teaspoonful soda, two of cream tartar, a little salt.

CORN CAKE No. 3. (Old Fashioned.)

One cup sweet milk, one cup molasses, one teaspoonful soda, two teaspoonfuls cream tartar : mix thin with Indian meal and a little flour.

BREAKFAST PUFFS.

One pint flour, one pint sweet milk, two eggs, lump of butter size of a walnut. Bake in gem pans.

RICE WAFFLES.

Boil one cup of rice; when cold, mix with two cups flour, two eggs, one tablespoonful sugar, half cup yeast, a little salt, water to thin; let rise over night.

POP-OVERS.

Three cups milk, three cups flour, three eggs. Bake half an hour in a quick oven, in gem pans.

BISCUIT.

One cup milk, one tablespoonful butter, one teaspoonful soda, two of cream tartar; mix very soft, mould very lightly, and cut into shape. This makes nine biscuit.

SALLIE LUNN.

One egg, butter size of a butternut, half cup sugar; beat these together; teacup sweet milk, two cups flour, three teaspoonfuls baking powder; bake twenty-five minutes.

CORN FRITTERS No. 1.

One pint grated corn, one gill cream, two cups flour, two eggs, one teaspoonful salt; fry in salt pork fat.

CORN FRITTERS No. 2.

One egg beaten, three tablespoonfuls flour, butter size of a walnut, a little salt, six ears of corn cut off and chopped fine, milk enough to thin; fry in salt pork fat.

FRITTERS.

To one pint sour milk add a little salt, one half teaspoonful soda, one egg; stir in flour enough for a batter, not too stiff.

CREAM FRITTERS.

Mix one and one half pints of flour with a pint of milk, stir in five well beaten eggs, add one half nutmeg, two teaspoonfuls salt, one pint cream ; stir the whole just enough to intermix the cream, add a few tender apples chopped fine, then fry in small cakes.

STRAWBERRY SHORTCAKE No. 1.

One cup milk, butter the size of an egg, pinch of salt, one teaspoonful soda, two teaspoonfuls cream tartar, flour enough to mould lightly ; bake in a quick oven ; when done, split open ; mash three pints of strawberries with powdered sugar, butter the cake and fill with the berries.

STRAWBERRY SHORTCAKE No. 2.

One cup sugar, one half cup butter, one half cup milk, two eggs, one and one half cups flour, one half teaspoonful soda, one teaspoonful cream tartar. Bake in two round tins : when done, spread mashed sweetened strawberries between layers, and on top whole berries with whipped cream over them.

ORANGE SHORTCAKE.

One egg, one cup milk, two tablespoonfuls melted butter, one heaping teaspoonful baking powder : make as stiff as pound cake ; bake on round tins : when done, split open ; cut up eight oranges in small bits, and prepare the same as strawberry shortcake.

SOUPS

"Some like it hot,
Some like it cold,
Some like it in the pot,
Nine days old."

STOCK FOR SOUP.

Take lean beef and cold water, in proportion of one pound of beef to one quart water; place it in a soup kettle over a good fire ; when it boils, add a cup of cold water and remove the scum; then place the kettle over a moderate fire, and let it simmer slowly four or five hours. This stock may be used for all soups in which meat broth is desired. It will make a good soup by adding canned tomatoes, and serving with small pieces of toasted bread.

BEEF SOUP.

Take sufficient soup stock ; boil one onion, one carrot, one quart of potatoes, and vegetables to suit taste, in a little water, and strain into the soup stock : add pepper, salt, etc., to suit.

BOUILLON SOUP.

Put a shank of beef (six or seven pounds) into a large pot and cover with cold water; leave on front of stove until it boils, then move it to the back of stove and let it simmer an hour and a half; cut up two carrots, two onions, and half a lemon : salt to taste, and boil until the meat falls from the bones; then strain through a sieve and set in the cold.

Next day remove every particle of grease that has risen to the top, heat the bouillon and pour into cups, first having a slice of lemon in each cup; season to taste.

TOMATO SOUP.

One pint of cooked tomatoes, one pint of water; when boiled, add half teaspoonful soda; when done foaming, add one quart hot milk; season good with butter, pepper, and salt.

❧ FISH ❧

" With hooks and nets you catch us,
  You never regard our pains;
  Yet we reward you with dainty food,
  To strengthen your body and brains."

CLAM CHOWDER.

One quart of clams squeezed. Fry two slices of pork in an iron pot. Slice two onions and eight potatoes; put in a layer of potatoes and onions, then add a layer of broken crackers, sprinkle with pepper and salt; fill up the remainder in this way, cook until the potatoes are done, the last-half hour putting in the clams. Just before serving add one pint hot milk.

CODFISH BALLS.

Three pints of boiling water, one cup salt codfish which has been picked into small pieces and freed from bones, one pint of potatoes peeled and quartered. Put all together in a pan, and boil until the potatoes are soft. Drain off the water, mash and beat until soft and smooth, add one teaspoonful butter, a little pepper, and when slightly cooled, add one well-beaten egg. Shape into balls, fry in hot lard.

PARSNIP BALLS. (F. M.)

Boil in salted water until tender; mash, and season with butter, pepper, and salt; add a little flour and two well-beaten eggs: form into small balls, and fry in hot lard.

LITTLE PIGS IN BLANKETS.

Take large oysters, wrap each one in a slice of bacon, cut very thin; fasten with little wooden toothpicks, roll in beaten egg, then in cracker dust, and fry quickly in a hot spider.

TURBOUT.

Three pounds of halibut steamed until tender; remove bones and sprinkle with salt and pepper. Dressing. — Heat one quart of milk and thicken with one fourth pound flour; when cool add two eggs and one fourth pound of butter; put in the baking dish a layer of fish, cover with sauce, then another layer of fish, and so on until all is used; season with parsley, cover the top with bread crumbs, bake half an hour.

CODFISH DIP.

Soak the fish in lukewarm water over night; boil one quart of milk, thicken with two tablespoonfuls flour, then add two cups shredded codfish; boil all together; serve with mashed potatoes.

CODFISH BALLS.

One pound codfish soaked over night, four large potatoes; place potatoes in a kettle of boiling water, and codfish in colander and set it over the potatoes (when the potatoes are tender the fish will be sufficiently steamed); then mash potatoes, pick codfish in pieces, add a large piece of butter, two tablespoonfuls cream, one egg, beat all together, roll in balls and fry.

CORN FISH.

One pint grated green corn, one half cup sweet milk, one egg, one tablespoonful sour cream or a little butter, a little salt, flour to make as stiff as batter cake; fry in the shape of oysters, in half butter, suet, or lard.

BAKED FISH.

A fish weighing from four to six pounds is good size to bake. Make a dressing of bread crumbs, butter, salt, and a little salt pork, chopped fine, (parsley and onions if you wish); mix this with one egg; fill the body, sew it up and lay it in a large dripper; put across it some strips of salt pork; bake one and a half hours.

CREAM SAUCE FOR FISH.

Heat a cup of milk to scalding; stir into it a teaspoonful of corn starch wet up with a little water; when this thickens, add two tablespoonfuls butter, with pepper, salt, and chopped parsley; beat an egg light, pour the sauce gradually over it; put it again over the fire and stir one minute, and pour over the fish.

FISH CROQUETTES.

Take cold fish left from dinner, pick in small pieces, add one third potato, season, roll in balls, dip in egg, and then in cracker crumbs. Fry in lard; add an egg if desired.

OYSTERS ESCALLOPED.

One quart oysters, one quart bowl cream bread crusts, one large tablespoonful butter, teaspoonful salt and pepper, one cup milk.

STEAMED OYSTERS.

One quart oysters for six or seven persons; put this quantity into a two-quart dish, with a small piece of butter, a little salt, and a little milk: place in the steamer and let it steam twenty minutes after the water begins to boil. They will be delicious.

CREAMED OYSTERS.

One pint milk boiled; one pint oysters (liquor strained), three tablespoonfuls flour to thicken; when cooked, serve with buttered toast.

MEATS

"Cheerful looks make every dish a feast,
And 'tis that crowns a welcome."

ROAST LAMB AND MINT SAUCE.

Stuff a hind quarter of lamb with fine bread crumbs, pepper, salt, and butter; rub the outside with salt, pepper, butter, flour; then roast two hours. Mint Sauce. — Chop the mint fine; pour on a little hot water; let it stand on the stove a short time, then add a little vinegar and sugar to taste.

HAM BALLS.

Chop fine cold cooked ham; add an egg for each person, and a little flour; beat together, make into balls, and fry in hot butter.

HASH.

Hash made of two parts potato, one part corned beef, and one part beets, is an appetizing dish for breakfast. The potatoes and beets should be boiled the day before : chop, season with butter, pepper, and salt.

VEAL PATÉ.

Three-and-a-half-pound leg of veal chopped raw, six small crackers rolled fine, three eggs, small pieces of butter, one tablespoonful salt, one tablespoonful nutmeg, one teaspoonful pepper, one small slice of pork chopped fine : mix all together into a loaf; put bits of butter on top, and grated bread crumbs over all; put in the oven with a little water : baste often; bake two hours, and when cold cut in thin slices.

BAKED HAM.

Boil four hours; take off skin and rub a heaping table-spoonful white sugar into the rind, and stick it with whole cloves. Bake it, basting with vinegar and water.

MOTHER'S BROIL FOR STEAK.

Heat a griddle very hot; lay on the beefsteak, and lift it up again quickly, and repeat until the steak ceases to stick to the griddle ; then turn and treat in the same way until the steak is cooked as desired. Have ready a heated dish ; salt and pepper the meat on both sides, and butter, pressing with a knife and fork to bring the juice. This is as good as broiling on the gridiron, if attended to.

FRIED TRIPE. (O. A. K.)

Dredge with flour, and fry in hot butter until a delicate brown on both sides. Serve on very hot dishes. In buying tripe, get the "honeycomb," as it is the best.

BEEFSTEAK TOAST.

Chop cold steak very fine ; cook in a little water, put in cream or milk ; thicken, season with butter, salt, pepper. Serve on buttered toast.

TO COOK AN OLD FOWL.

Dress and stuff as for roasting; boil three hours in a covered pot with one quart water, to which add two table-spoonfuls vinegar; then take from the water, rub over with butter, sprinkle on some flour, and bake an hour. Use the liquid to baste with, and for gravy. The vinegar makes the fowl tender, but does not taste at all.

CHICKEN CROQUETTES.

To any quantity of cold chicken add one third as much potato; chop fine and season; add enough chicken gravy to moisten it; two eggs well beaten for one chicken; make into balls, drop into beaten egg, then in cracker crumbs, and fry in hot lard until brown.

BAKED CHICKEN.

Dress the chickens, cut them in two, soak half an hour in cold water, wipe perfectly dry, and put in a dripping-pan, bone side down, without any water; have a hot oven, and if the chickens are young, half an hour's cooking will be sufficient. Take out and season with butter, pepper, and salt; boil the giblets in a little water, and after the chickens are taken from the pan, put into it the water in which the giblets were boiled, thicken, and add chopped giblets.

PRESSED CHICKEN.

Boil chicken very tender: be sure to have plenty of liquor; separate white meat from the dark: soak three slices of bread in the liquor for a few minutes, then chop it up with the dark meat. Put white meat in the bottom of the dish, pour a little liquor on, then put on a layer of dark meat; leave until it is cold, and it will turn out like jelly.

POT ROAST.

Take a lean piece of beef: fry two slices of salt pork in an iron pot a few minutes; season the beef and sprinkle over a little flour, then put in the pot and fry brown on all sides. Pour in hot water to half cover the beef, cover tightly and cook until tender: add a little boiling water at intervals to prevent burning: thicken the gravy and pour around the meat on the platter. Meats to be roasted or broiled should be given the greatest amount of heat possible at first, that the surface may be hardened and the juices retained.

CHICKEN PIE.

Boil two chickens in salted water, just enough to cover them, until done; then put the chicken in the dish in layers — salt, pepper, and butter each layer, dredge in a little flour, and cover with a light crust. Put in enough of the liquor in which the meat was boiled to cover the meat. Bake one hour.

BROILED PORK STEAK.

These should be cut thin, broiled quick, and very thoroughly.

TURKEY WITH OYSTER DRESSING.

For a ten-pound turkey take two pints bread crumbs, half a teacupful butter cut in small pieces, one teaspoonful summer savory, pepper and salt; rub the turkey with flour, pepper, and salt. Fill the turkey with a teaspoonful of dressing, a few well strained oysters, alternating until filled. Put the oyster liquid in the pan with a pint of water; bake in a moderate oven.

FRIED BREAD FOR SOUP.

Cut bread into little squares about three fourths of an inch thick; fry in butter, turning the pieces, so that every piece will be browned.

CREAM CHICKEN.

Place one half pint rich cream over the fire, with two tablespoonfuls chopped parsley, a dash of cayenne pepper, and salt to taste; cut the white meat into small pieces, enough to fill a pint measure; after the cream is hot, stir in the chicken, and continue stirring for two minutes; serve in patty shells.

TARTARE SAUCE.

Half pint Mayonnaise dressing, two teaspoonfuls chopped capers, two teaspoonfuls chopped olives, one teaspoonful chopped cucumber pickles, one teaspoonful chopped parsley ; mix well. This sauce is nice for broiled fish.

CREAM CHICKEN.

One pint of chicken which has been boiled ; mix with two parts bread crumbs wet with cream ; fill patty shells, sprinkle the top with cracker crumbs and bits of butter ; season with salt and pepper, then bake.

DELICIOUS CREAMED CHICKEN.

Place one pint of cream over the fire ; thicken with a little flour, then add the chicken cut in small pieces, seasoned with pepper, salt, and a little wine. Fill the patty shells with the mixture, then cover with rolled cracker and melted butter ; bake a light brown. Fish done in this way is very nice.

☙ SALADS ❧

To make a perfect salad there should be a miser for oil, a spend-thrift for vinegar, a wise man for salt, and a madcap to stir the ingredients up and mix them well together.— *Spanish Proverb.*

LOBSTER SALAD. (M. F. W.)

Four eggs, óne tablespoonful sugar, two tablespoonfuls butter, one teaspoonful salt, two tablespoonfuls vinegar, one tablespoonful mustard; beat the whites of the eggs separately, and last cook in a bowl of water, stirring until it thickens; when cold, add cream enough to make thin as boiled custard; add salt and red pepper to the chopped lobster.

OYSTER SALAD

Is made by cooking oysters in as little water as possible to use; drain this off when they are done, and pour over them a regular salad dressing. If you choose you may sprinkle over this celery chopped fine.

CHICKEN SALAD.

Equal parts of cold boiled chicken, and celery cut in small pieces with a sharp knife. Pour over this a salad dressing.

SALMON SALAD.

One small can of salmon, boned and picked over fine, one head of lettuce chopped. Take the yolks of two eggs, one half cupful vinegar, butter size of an egg, one teaspoonful sugar, one half teaspoonful red pepper, one teaspoonful salt, one half teaspoonful mustard; put on the fire, stirring until it boils; remove from the fire and add one half cupful cream; boil three eggs hard, add two eggs to the salmon, reserving one to garnish the dish.

CABBAGE SALAD.

One head white cabbage chopped fine; when done, pour over a regular salad dressing.

SALAD DRESSING No. 1.

Into four tablespoonfuls of melted butter smooth one tablespoonful flour, add one cup milk and bring it to a boil. Beat together four eggs, two tablespoonfuls sugar, one of salt, one of mustard, and a small quantity of red pepper; add three fourths of a cupful of vinegar; pour into the hot milk and allow it to thicken to the consistency of cream; strain and cool.

SALAD DRESSING No. 2.

The yolk of a raw egg well beaten; add one fourth tea- spoonful salt, pinch of red pepper; drop by drop pour in a pint of best salad oil, stirring constantly; if too thick, thin with vinegar or lemon juice to the consistency of cream; finally add some capers.

POTATO SALAD.

One quart cold potatoes, one onion, a little parsley, one beet; cut the potato in small pieces, chop the onion, beet, and parsley fine, and pour over the whole Salad Dressing No. 1.

MAYONNAISE DRESSING.

The yolks of three uncooked eggs, one tablespoonful mustard, one half tablespoonful sugar, one teaspoonful salt, juice of half a lemon, one half cup of vinegar, a pint of oil, and a cupful of whipped cream. Beat the yolks, mustard, sugar, and salt, until very light, adding a few drops of oil at a time until the dressing becomes thick; add oil and vinegar until all are used; then add the juice of the lemon, the whipped cream, and a thought of cayenne pepper; place on ice until ready to use.

WELSH RAREBIT.

One half pound cheese cut in small pieces; a piece of butter size of an egg put in the frying-pan; lay in the cheese for about five minutes, add two eggs well beaten, a teaspoonful of mixed mustard, pepper, and salt; have ready several slices of toast, turn the cheese over it, and send to the table hot.

DRAWN BUTTER.

One half cup butter rubbed *well* with two tablespoonfuls flour; put into a saucepan with about a pint of boiling water, stirring constantly until melted; throw in a little parsley, and serve.

OYSTER SAUCE.

To drawn butter sauce add a pint of oysters drained from their liquor, and a few drops of vinegar. Let it come to a boil, and serve.

⚜ VEGETABLES ⚜

"Better is a dinner of herbs where love is, than a stalled ox and hatred therewith."

ASPARAGUS ON TOAST.

Wash and cut off the tough part. Put the remainder in salted boiling water; boil from ten to fifteen minutes; drain, season with salt, pepper, and butter, and pour over slices of buttered toast.

EGG PLANT.

Cut in thin slices and soak in cold salted water about two hours. Just before time to serve, dry in towels; dip each piece in egg and dredge with rolled cracker; fry to a delicate brown (in lard); serve as soon as fried, or it will not be crisp.

WHIPPED POTATOES.

Boil required number of potatoes; add salt, pepper, butter, and milk; whip to a cream with a fork.

CREAMED POTATOES.

Put one tablespoonful butter in frying-pan, and when it bubbles, add one tablespoonful flour, one cup hot milk, with salt and pepper to taste, one pint cold potatoes cut into small dice, one half onion; cook until done.

EGGS

BOILED EGGS.

Put them into water that boils. If you like them very soft, boil them three minutes; if you wish the yolk hard, boil five minutes.

FRIED EGGS.

After you have fried ham, drop in the eggs one at a time: in about a minute dip the boiling fat over them until done.

DROPPED EGGS.

Drop fresh eggs into a saucepan of boiling water with salt in it; have ready slices of buttered toast; then take up with a skimmer, and lay on the toast.

EGGS A LA CREAM.

Boil ten eggs until hard; slice in rings; in the bottom of a baking-dish place a layer of bread crumbs, then one of eggs; cover with bits of butter, pepper, and salt, until all are used; pour over them a cup of cream, and brown in the oven.

OMELET.

Beat six eggs very light, the whites to a froth, the yolks to a batter; add to the yolks a cupful of milk, a little pepper and salt; add the whites last, lightly; have ready in a hot frying-pan a good lump of butter; when it hisses, pour the mixture in gently; it should cook ten minutes; do not stir it, but when it begins to "set" slip a knife under it to prevent it burning on the bottom.

ᕦ PUDDINGS ᕤ

"Expectation whirls me round;
Th' imaginary relish is so sweet
That it enchants my sense."

TAPIOCA PUDDING.

Soak eight tablespoonfuls tapioca in a quart of warm milk till soft; then add two tablespoonfuls melted butter, five eggs well beaten, spice, sugar, and wine to your taste; bake in a buttered dish without any lining.

HUCKLEBERRY PUDDING.

One cup molasses, one and one half pints berries, one and one half pints flour, one teaspoonful soda, one half teaspoonful salt; steam one and one half hours; liquid sauce.

DELICIOUS PUDDING.

Two slices cake, one cup sugar, two eggs, one quart milk, cup raisins, nutmeg and cinnamon to taste; bake one hour.

BROWN BETTY.

Put a layer of sweetened apple sauce in a buttered dish; add a few lumps of butter, then a layer of cracker crumbs sprinkled with a little cinnamon, then a layer of sauce, etc., making the last layer of crumbs; bake in oven, and eat hot with cold sweetened cream.

BREAD PUDDING.

One quart sweet milk, quart bread crumbs, four eggs, four tablespoonfuls sugar; soak bread in half the milk until soft; mash fine; add rest of the milk, the well-beaten eggs and sugar, and a teacupful raisins; bake one hour; serve warm, with warm ·sauce.

COCOANUT BREAD PUDDING.

Soak one cup of cocoanut in one pint milk; boil; as soon as it boils, add one pint cold milk thickened with one tablespoonful corn starch or one powdered cracker, little butter, salt, three beaten eggs; then add nutmeg and sugar to taste.

STEAMED BREAD PUDDING.

Two cups bread crumbs soaked in a little water to soften, one cup molasses, four full tablespoonfuls flour, one egg, one teaspoonful soda, two of cream tartar, fruit and spice to taste; steam three hours; eat with wine sauce.

A DISH OF SNOW.

Grate the white part of a cocoanut; put in a glass dish, and serve with currant or cranberry jellies.

PORK PUDDING.

One cup sour milk, one cup molasses, one cup pork chopped fine, one teaspoonful soda; mix quite stiff and steam two hours; serve hot with sauce.

DELMONICO PUDDING.

One quart milk, one cup white sugar; let this boil, then stir in four tablespoonfuls corn starch which has been dissolved in a little milk, the yolks of six eggs well beaten; bake twenty minutes. Beat the whites of the eggs nearly stiff, and add to them six tablespoonfuls white sugar; pour this over the pudding, set in the oven until a delicate brown.

APPLE TAPIOCA PUDDING.

One cup tapioca cooked over the fire in four cups water; add four apples quartered, one cup sugar; season with cinnamon, lemon, and salt; add a small piece of butter; bake slowly until done. Serve with rich cream.

WHITE WINE PUDDING.

Cut sponge cake into thin slices and line a deep dish; make it moist with white wine; make a rich custard, using only the yolks of the eggs; when cool, turn it into the dish, and beat the whites to a stiff froth and spread on top.

BLUEBERRY PUDDING.

One pint milk, three eggs, three pints berries; if berries are fresh, make thin batter with flour; if soft, make it thick. Steam one and one half hours in mould.

TO BOIL RICE.

Wash the rice thoroughly with cold water, then throw into a saucepan of boiling water well salted; let it boil till the grains soften; then pour the water off, cover closely to steam, and set back on the stove, where it remains until the grains separate from each other. To half a pound of rice use about three pints of water.

PLAIN BAKED INDIAN PUDDING.

Scald two quarts sweet milk; into which stir ten rounded tablespoonfuls Indian meal, seven tablespoonfuls molasses, one teaspoonful ginger, and a little salt. Put in moderate oven to bake, and in half an hour stir in half cup cold milk; bake in a very slow oven four hours, and a longer time will not injure it. Serve with cream or hot sauce.

DELICIOUS LEMON PUDDING.

The juice and grated rind of one lemon, one cup sugar, yolks of two eggs, three tablespoonfuls flour, and milk enough to fill the dish; line dish with paste, pour in custard, and bake till done; beat whites of two eggs, add four tablespoonfuls sugar, spread on top, and brown.

QUEEN PUDDING.

One pint bread crumbs, one quart milk, yolks of four eggs, one lemon, sugar to taste; bake like custard; after baking, spread with jelly, then frost and brown; liquid sauce.

FLUMMERY.

Bake six large apples very soft; beat the whites of two eggs to a stiff froth; then beat the soft part of the apple in with it, and sweeten to taste. To be eaten cold for tea.

PUDDING.

One pint chocolate or coffee strained, half box gelatine, one cup sugar, yolks of four eggs; place all things in a pan; stir until steam issues; when cold, add one pint whipped cream; pour in moulds and serve when cold.

FAVORITE PUDDING.

Bake common sponge cake in a flat-bottomed pudding-dish; when desired for use, cut it into sixths or eighths, split each piece, butter them, and return them to their places in the dish. Make a custard with four eggs to one quart milk; season, sweeten to the taste, and pour it over the cake; bake half an hour; the cake will swell and fill the custard.

ENGLISH PUDDING.

Two eggs, one cup milk, one cup molasses, one cup raisins, three cups flour, one teaspoonful soda; steam three hours.

BAKED RICE PUDDING.

One quart milk, four tablespoonfuls rice, five table-spoonfuls sugar, salt, one egg; bake three hours.

SUET PUDDING.

One cup chopped suet, one cup molasses, one cup sour milk, one cup raisins, four cups flour, one teaspoonful salt, one teaspoonful soda; boil three hours.

SNOW AND ICE PUDDING.

Half a box of gelatine, one and a half pints boiling water, two cups sugar, juice of two lemons; strain and set away to cool; make a soft custard of one pint milk, two eggs, one teaspoonful corn starch, two tablespoonfuls sugar, a little salt; when served, cut the jelly in small squares, put in a glass dish, and pour the custard over it.

COCOANUT PUDDING.

Grate one cocoanut into one quart milk, three eggs, seven tablespoonfuls sugar, little salt, one teaspoonful flavoring.

ORANGE PUDDING.

Peel and cut into thin slices six oranges; pour over them one coffee cup white sugar and let them stand over night; in the morning take a pint of boiling milk, add the yolks of three eggs well beaten, one tablespoonful corn starch made smooth with a little milk; stir constantly; when cool, pour over the oranges: leave the whites for frosting.

INDIAN PUDDING.

One quart milk, one cup flour, one cup Indian meal, one cup molasses, one cup sugar, one cup butter, two eggs, one teaspoonful salt; scald the Indian meal and flour with part of the milk; when it commences to thicken, remove from the fire; add the remainder of the milk cold, with the other ingredients; bake slowly two hours.

COTTAGE PUDDING.

One cup sugar, one tablespoonful butter, two eggs, one cup sweet milk, three cups flour, one half teaspoonful soda, one teaspoonful cream tartar sifted with the flour, one teaspoonful salt; eat with a liquid sauce.

FRUIT PUDDING.

One pint flour, one pint fruit, one teacup molasses, one teaspoonful soda stirred in the molasses, one teaspoonful salt; steam two hours. The fruit can be green, or dried, or canned; pudding steamed or baked.

IMPROMPTU DESSERT.

Cover the bottom of a large glass dish with sliced orange; strew over it powdered sugar, then a thick layer of cocoanut; alternate orange and cocoanut till the dish is full, heaping cocoanut on top.

COFFEE JELLY.

One half box gelatine soaked in one half pint cold water; add one pint strong coffee mixed with one half pint boiling water and one and a half cups sugar; let it just come to a boil, then strain; this should be served with cream, either whipped, frozen, or plain, cold.

PINEAPPLE SHERBET.

One pineapple grated, or one can of pineapple, one pint cold water, one pint sugar, one tablespoonful gelatine dissolved in the water; mix together and freeze.

ORANGES JELLIED.

Six large oranges; cut a hole in the top of each, large enough to admit the bowl of a small spoon, and carefully remove all the juice and pulp; take the juice of one lemon, the orange pulp, one and a half cups sugar, one half box gelatine, and one half cup cold water; soak together for half an hour; place all in a sauce-pan, pour in a cup of boiling water, and let stand on the stove until the mixture is well dissolved; strain through a bag; fill the orange skins, put on the tops, and set away to cool and harden; the next day cut each orange in two with a very sharp knife; serve one half orange to each person.

ITALIAN CREAM.

One half box gelatine, one quart milk, yolks of three eggs, three large tablespoonfuls sugar; cook all together in a boiler; beat the whites stiff and pour the custard over them; beat all together; two tablespoonfuls flavoring; turn into moulds to cool.

NELLIE RUSSE.

Soak one fourth package gelatine in one pint milk one hour; put on the stove and let it come to a boil; stir in the beaten yolks of three eggs, with half cup sugar; cook till it thickens, then take off the stove and stir in lightly the whites beaten to a stiff froth.

WHIPPED CREAM.

One and a half pints good rich cream sweetened and flavored to taste, three teaspoonfuls vanilla; whip to a stiff froth; dissolve three fourths of an ounce best gelatine in a small teacupful hot water, and when cool pour into the cream; stir thoroughly; pour into moulds and set on ice, or in a very cool place.

STRAWBERRY CREAM.

One quart strawberries rubbed through a hair sieve ; mix with three pints rich cream, and sweeten ; whip to a froth, and add half an ounce dissolved gelatine.

TAPIOCA FLOAT.

Four tablespoonfuls tapioca soaked over night in a little water; in the morning add one cup sugar, three eggs, and a little salt; heat the milk, add the tapioca, and boil twenty minutes; beat the yolks of the eggs with the sugar, add the salt, and stir into the milk ; boil five minutes ; pour into a dish ; beat the whites of the eggs to a stiff froth, then add two tablespoonfuls sugar; frost, and set in the oven until a delicate brown.

FRUIT HARLEQUIN.

One pineapple pared and sliced thin, one box strawberries, four oranges sliced, a half dozen bananas sliced ; put in a sauce dish a layer of pineapple, one of strawberries, one of oranges, one of bananas, then one of strawberries ; sprinkle each layer with sugar, and over the whole squeeze the juice of a lemon ; prepare this in the morning, and it will be ready for tea.

FROZEN PEACHES.

One quart milk, four eggs ; beat the yolks and one and a half cups of sugar; scald the milk and stir the yolks and sugar into it ; remove when thick and put in the whites of the eggs, well beaten ; when cold, stir in a quart of cream, then a quart of either fresh or preserved peaches rubbed through a sieve ; place in a freezer and freeze.

PEACHES AND CREAM.

Peel, slice, and heap up in a glass dessert dish, and serve raw with fine sugar and cream.

STRAWBERRY JELLY.

Soak one box gelatine in half a pint cold water twenty minutes; add one pint boiling water; stir until dissolved; add a cup of sugar, strained juice of one and a half pints strawberries, and juice of one lemon.

FLOATING ISLAND.

One quart milk, six eggs (whites and yolks beaten separately), five tablespoonfuls (heaping) white sugar, two tablespoonfuls extract bitter almond or vanilla, half a cup currant jelly; beat the yolks well, stir in the sugar, and add the hot (not boiling) milk, a little at a time: boil until it begins to thicken; when cool, flavor and pour into a glass dish, first stirring it up well: heap upon it a meringue of the whites, into which you have beaten gradually half a cup currant jelly; dot with bits of jelly cut into rings or straight slips.

LEMON JELLY.

Soak half a box gelatine one hour in half a pint water; add the juice of three lemons and one pound sugar: pour on one pint boiling water, strain through a cloth, and let it stand over night; never fails.

CHARLOTTE RUSSE.

Line two medium sized moulds with cake; then beat two eggs, put in a teacupful pulverized sugar, flavor to taste; whip a pint sweet cream; have a third of a package of gelatine soaked in a cup of milk; put all together and pour into moulds: let it stand a little while before ready for eating.

MAY'S PEACH PUDDING.

One pint canned peaches frosted with the whites of four eggs; put into the oven and brown; serve with rich cream and powdered sugar.

FROZEN PUDDING.

Make a soft custard of eight eggs and one quart milk, leaving out the whites of four of the eggs; add one half cup currants, one half cup raisins, one half cup sliced citron; let it cool, and add candied or preserved cherries, strawberries, a little raspberry jam, one pint whipped cream, the whipped whites of the eggs, and sugar to taste; freeze.

SPANISH CREAM.

Soak one third of a box of gelatine two hours in a gill of cold milk taken from a quart, and set in a cool place; then stir the gelatine into the remainder of the milk, which must be boiling. Have in readiness a cream made of a teacupful sugar well beaten into three eggs and seasoned with a pinch of salt: stir this into the liquid until the latter almost, but not quite boils: remove from the fire and beat in any flavoring desired (a teaspoonful of some good extract being sufficient). Strain through soup sieve into a wet mould, and set in a cool place. Serve with sugar and cream, or with any cold liquid sauce.

BAKED INDIAN PUDDING.

One quart milk, one scant cup Indian meal, one half cup molasses, two eggs, butter size of an egg, one teaspoonful cinnamon, a little salt, and ginger; wet the meal with cold water and pour the boiling milk over it; when cold, add the other ingredients, and bake half an hour.

BERNIE'S SHERBET.

One pint sugar, juice of two lemons, beaten together; one teaspoonful extract of lemon; pour into the freezer and add one quart rich milk; then freeze.

ORANGE CREAM.

One pint cream, one pint milk, one cup sugar, two eggs; flavor with orange and vanilla; freeze.

ICE CREAM.

Take three pints milk and bring to a boil; add six eggs well beaten with two cups of sugar; stir until it thickens like soft custard; when cool, add one quart cream and one cup sugar; flavor and freeze.

FROZEN PEACHES.

Take one quart peaches, peeled and sliced; sprinkle with half a pound of sugar, and let stand two hours; mash fine, add one quart cold water, and freeze the same as ice cream.

STRAWBERRY OR RASPBERRY CREAM.

Bruise a pint of raspberries or strawberries with two large tablespoonfuls fine sugar; add a quart of cream; strain through a sieve, and freeze it.

RICH CREAM.

Squeeze a dozen lemons and strain the juice upon as much fine sugar as it will absorb; pour three quarts cream into it very slowly, stirring very fast all the time.

⚜ PUDDING SAUCES ⚜

"To be good, be useful. To be useful, always be making something good."

WHITE SAUCE.

One cup sugar, one egg — white and yolk beaten separately; beat the sugar and yolk together; add four tablespoonfuls boiling milk, and lastly the beaten white of the egg.

EGG SAUCE.

Two eggs, half a teacupful sugar, three tablespoonfuls boiling water; flavoring; beat long and hard.

STRAWBERRY SAUCE.

Beat half a cup butter to a cream; add one cup powdered sugar and the beaten white of an egg; then beat in two cups of berries.

HARD SAUCE.

Beat butter and sugar to a cream; add the white of one egg beaten to a froth, and flavor.

LEMON SAUCE.

One cup sugar, half a cup butter, one egg, one lemon (the juice and grated rind), one teaspoonful nutmeg, three tablespoonfuls boiling water; cream the butter and sugar; beat in the egg whipped light, the lemon and nutmeg; beat hard, and add a teaspoonful at a time to the boiling water;

put into a tin pail and set into the uncovered top of the tea-kettle, which must be kept boiling until the steam heats the sauce very hot, but not to boiling; stir constantly.

EGG SAUCE.

One egg well beaten, one cup powdered sugar, three tablespoonfuls boiled milk; flavor.

FOAMING SAUCE.

One half cup butter, one half cup sugar, one half cup wine (hot), one egg; beat together butter and sugar, break the egg and beat it to a foam, beating all one way; then stir in wine hot, and melt on the stove. Be careful not to let it boil.

VINEGAR SAUCE.

One and a half cups sugar, one and a half tablespoon-fuls flour in a little water, two tablespoonfuls vinegar, quarter of a grated nutmeg, and a pinch of salt; pour over this one and a half pints boiling water, and boil ten minutes; just before taking from the stove add one tablespoonful butter.

WHIPPED CREAM SAUCE.

Whip a pint of rich cream, add the beaten whites of two eggs, sweeten to taste, and flavor.

PASTRY

"An't please your honour," quoth the peasant,
"This same dessert is very pleasant." — *Pope.*

PIE CRUST.

Take four cups pastry flour, one cup lard, and one half teaspoonful salt; work the lard into the flour with a knife until it is fine like meal. Mix with ice water, pouring on a little at a time, until enough water has been added to wet it together. Put the dough upon the board and flatten; when half an inch thick, put on small bits of lard, sprinkle on a little flour, cut into four strips; pile one upon the other, placing the last one bottom side up; with the rolling pin pound briskly; roll again, sprinkle with lard and flour, pound, then roll up as you would for jelly cake, and it is ready to use.

APPLE PIE.

Pare and cut into slices; place a row of slices around the plate one half inch from the edge; fill the center, putting on the top slices evenly; sprinkle on a little salt, cinnamon, nutmeg, and a cup of sugar, with pieces of butter. Before putting into the oven wet the crust with milk.

GRANDMA'S APPLE PUFFS.

Pare and stew four apples; when done, add sugar, nutmeg, and lemon to taste. Make a rich crust, roll thin, cut in squares, fill with the apple, sprinkle with sugar. Bake a light brown.

LEMON PIE.

One cup hot water, one tablespoonful corn starch, one cup sugar, one tablespoonful butter, the juice and grated rind of one lemon ; cook for a few moments : add one egg, and bake with top and bottom crust.

CORA'S LEMON PIE.

Two eggs, one and a half cups sugar, the juice and rind of two lemons, a small piece of butter, two tablespoonfuls flour, one fourth cup water, a little salt. Bake in two crusts.

CURRANT PIE.

One cup ripe currants, one cup sugar, one egg : beat well together, and bake between two crusts.

HOTEL PIE.

Let two cupfuls of water come to a boil, then put in two tablespoonfuls corn starch dissolved in a little milk ; when it has boiled enough, take from the stove, add the juice and rind of two lemons, two cupfuls sugar, a piece of butter size of a nutmeg, and the yolks of two eggs ; use the whites for frosting.

COCOANUT PIE.

One pint milk, one cup cocoanut, one tablespoonful corn starch, three eggs ; sweeten to taste. Make a meringue of the whites of the eggs and four tablespoonfuls powdered sugar.

LEMON MERINGUE PIE.

Two lemons, grate the rind, remove the skin, and chop the rest very fine ; into one cup hot water stir well one tablespoonful corn starch, and boil ; when cool, add one cup sugar, yolks of three eggs, and the chopped lemon ; stir well ; line one plate with crust, pour in the mixture ; when baked, cover with a meringue made with the whites of the eggs and three tablespoonfuls of sugar ; brown.

MINCE PIE.

Three bowls finely chopped meat, three bowls chopped apples, one bowl suet, one bowl of citron cut fine, two of raisins, four of sugar, one of molasses, one of boiled cider, one of some kind of preserve syrup; add one tablespoonful cinnamon, cloves, and mace, two nutmegs, one tablespoonful salt.

CREAM PIE.

One pint milk scalded, two tablespoonfuls corn starch, three tablespoonfuls sugar, yolks of two eggs; wet the starch in a little cold milk: beat the eggs and sugar until light, and stir the whole into the hot milk. Flavor with lemon or vanilla, and set aside to cool. Line a plate with pie crust and bake; when done, make a frosting with the whites of the eggs and a tablespoonful of sugar; brown.

WASHINGTON CREAM PIE.

Three eggs, one cup sugar, one cup flour, two tablespoonfuls cold water, two teaspoonfuls baking powder; beat all together five minutes; add salt, and flavor; when done, split open; whip a pint of cream and fill; this makes two pies.

CUSTARD PIE.

One pint milk, three eggs, half a tablespoonful corn starch, half cup sugar; strain and flavor.

RICH MINCE PIE.

Two pounds meat boiled, one half pound suet (boil it), two pounds currants, four pounds raisins, four pounds apples, four pounds sugar, one pound citron, two teaspoonfuls salt, two nutmegs, one half ounce cloves, cinnamon, juice of six lemons, one half pint rosewater; wet it well with vinegar, half pint brandy, one pint molasses. This will keep months.

WHIPPED CREAM PIE.

Three eggs, one cup sugar, one and a half cups flour, one half cup milk, two teaspoonfuls cream tartar, one teaspoonful soda. Makes two pies. Cream. — Two cups thick cream, one small cup powdered sugar, and one teaspoonful vanilla ; beat stiff.

SQUASH PIE.

One cup of squash sifted, one full half cup sugar, two eggs well beaten, one half teaspoonful salt, small piece butter; season with nutmeg, cinnamon, and ginger : milk enough to fill a pie of medium size.

CAKE

"She measured out the butter with a very solemn air;
 The milk and sugar also; and she took the greatest care
 To count her eggs correctly, and to add a little bit
 Of baking powder, which, you know, beginners oft omit.
 Then she stirred it all together, and she baked it full an hour;
 But she never quite forgave herself for leaving out the flour."
— *From Judge.*

WALNUT DROPS.

One cup of slightly chopped walnut meats, two eggs, one cup sugar, three tablespoonfuls flour; drop small spoonfuls in a buttered pan, several inches apart; bake in a quick oven.

MARBLED CAKE.

One cup butter, two cups powdered sugar, three cups flour, four eggs, one cup sweet milk, half a teaspoonful soda, one teaspoonful cream tartar sifted with the flour. When the cake is mixed, take out about a teacupful of the batter, and stir into this a great spoonful of grated chocolate wet with a scant tablespoonful of milk. Fill your mould about an inch deep with the yellow batter, and drop upon this in two or three places a spoonful of the dark mixture.

SPICE CAKE.

One cup butter, two cups sugar, three cups flour, four eggs, two tablespoonfuls sour milk, one teaspoonful soda, two teaspoonfuls cinnamon, one teaspoonful cloves and nutmeg, one cup raisins.

RAISIN SMASH.

Beat the whites of three eggs to a stiff froth, adding a cup and a half of pulverized sugar, a large cup of seedless chopped raisins, and a few blanched and minced almonds ; flavor with vanilla. For this icing prepare a cake as follows : Take two cups sugar, two of flour, and one of sweet milk ; add three teaspoonfuls of baking powder. Bake in two square tin pans. Place one layer over the other with the raisin smash icing, prepared as above, between them.

AUNT MARY'S FRUIT CAKE.

One cup butter, two cups sugar, three cups flour, five eggs, one half cup molasses, one half teaspoonful soda, two pounds raisins, one pound citron, one pound currants, two teaspoonfuls cinnamon, one teaspoonful cloves and nutmeg. Bake one and a half hours.

SILVER CAKE.

Two cups pulverized sugar, one cup butter, whites of six eggs, one half cup sweet milk, one teaspoonful baking powder. three light cups flour, or two and a half cups ; flavor.

GOLD CAKE.

One cup butter, yolks of six eggs and one whole one, one and a half cups sugar, one small half cup sweet milk, two and a half cups flour, one teaspoonful baking powder, or two of cream tartar and one of soda ; flavor.

MARBLE CAKE.

For the white cake. — One cup butter, three cups white sugar, five cups flour even full, one half cup sweet milk, one half teaspoonful soda, whites of eight eggs, flavor with lemon.

For the dark cake. — One cup butter, two cups brown sugar, one cup molasses, one cup sour milk, one teaspoonful soda, four cups flour, yolks of eight eggs, and one whole egg; spices of all kinds. Put in pans, first a layer of dark, then a layer of white, and so on, finishing with a dark layer. Bake in a hot oven.

ANGEL CAKE.

Whites of seven eggs beaten to a stiff froth, one cup sugar, two thirds cup flour, one half teaspoonful cream tartar sifted four times with the flour, one teaspoonful vanilla or lemon.

ELECTION CAKE.

One cup sugar, one half cup butter, one egg, one cup sweet milk, two and a half cups pastry flour, one cup stoned raisins, one teaspoonful soda, and one teaspoonful cinnamon and cloves.

ADDIE'S GOLD CAKE.

Two cups not quite full of flour, the yolks of four eggs, one cup sugar, one half cup butter, one half cup sweet milk, one half teaspoonful soda, one teaspoonful cream tartar. Flavor to taste.

"DOLLIE VARDEN'S" CAKE.

One cup sugar and one half cup butter beaten to a cream, whites of three eggs beaten to a froth, one half cup sweet milk, two cups flour, two teaspoonfuls baking powder; beat the yolks with fifteen teaspoonfuls of sugar, and put on top while hot for icing.

"MINUTE MAN" CAKE.

Two cups sugar, two thirds cup butter, whites of seven eggs well beaten, two thirds cup sweet milk, two cups flour, one cup maizena, two teaspoonfuls Royal baking powder. Bake in jelly tins.

FROSTING.

Whites of three eggs and sugar beaten together, not quite as stiff as usual frosting. Spread over the cake, then add grated cocoanut.

CHEAP RAISIN CAKE.

One cup sugar, one half cup molasses, one egg, piece butter size of an egg, three fourths cup rich butter-milk, coffee cup raisins, one teaspoonful soda, one teaspoonful cloves, one teaspoonful cinnamon.

SPONGE CAKE.

Six eggs, cup and a half of sugar, cup and a half of flour, a little salt, and flavoring.

CREAM SPONGE CAKE.

Beat two eggs in a coffee cup, fill the cup with cream, add one cup sugar, one of flour, one teaspoonful cream tartar, one half teaspoonful soda; flavor with lemon.

RIBBON CAKE.

One and a fourth cups sugar and half cup butter beaten together, three well-beaten eggs, two thirds cup sweet milk, two cups flour, one teaspoonful cream tartar, one half teaspoonful soda. Reserve two cups of this mixture for top and bottom cakes; to the remainder add one teaspoonful each of cinnamon and cloves, half a nutmeg, two tablespoonfuls molasses, one cup fruit, half cup flour. Bake in three cakes; place them together, the dark one in the centre, with jelly or frosting between; the top can be frosted if desired.

HOTEL COOKIES.

Two eggs, one cup sugar, one half cup butter, four tablespoonfuls milk, one teaspoonful cream tartar, one half teaspoonful soda, one tablespoonful caraway seeds; flour to roll.

WATER SPONGE.

Three eggs beaten four minutes; add one and a half cups sugar, beat one minute ; one cup flour, one half cup cold water, one cup flour, two teaspoonfuls cream tartar, one teaspoonful soda.

COCOANUT COOKIES.

One cup sugar, one half cup butter, one egg, one fourth cup milk, one cup cocoanut, one teaspoonful cream tartar, one half teaspoonful soda, flour to roll.

CREAM COOKIES.

Two cups sour cream, two cups sugar, one large teaspoonful soda, a little nutmeg and salt, flour to roll.

HARD SUGAR CAKES.

Two cups sugar, one cup butter (don't melt it), three eggs, one teaspoonful soda, three tablespoonfuls cold water ; roll thin, and bake quick.

IMPERIAL CAKE.

One pound sugar, one pound flour, three fourths pound butter, one pound almonds blanched and cut fine, one half pound citron, one half pound raisins stoned and cut in pieces, rind and juice of lemon, one nutmeg, ten eggs beaten separate.

FRUIT CAKE.

One pound butter, one pound sugar, one pound flour, three pounds raisins, three pounds currants, one pound citron, ten eggs, two wine glasses of brandy, two tablespoonfuls cloves and mace, one teaspoonful soda.

ADDIE'S CHOCOLATE JUMBLES.

One cup butter, two cups sugar, two cups grated chocolate, three cups flour, four eggs, teaspoonful soda, two teaspoonfuls cream tartar, a little salt; roll thin, and bake in a moderate oven.

FRUIT CAKE.

One cup butter, two cups sugar, one cup molasses, one cup milk, five eggs, five cups flour, one teaspoonful soda, spice of all kinds, one pound raisins, one pound currants, one half pound citron.

HELEN'S CAKE.

Four eggs, one and a half cups butter, one cup sugar, two cups molasses, one half cup sour milk, five cups flour, one heaping teaspoonful cinnamon, one teaspoonful cloves, one teaspoonful nutmeg; bake three hours.

ALMOND CAKE.

One half cup butter and two of sugar, three fourths cup sweet milk, two and a half cups flour, one teaspoonful soda, one heaping teaspoonful cream tartar, whites of six eggs, and one pound of blanched almonds.

ANGEL CAKE.

The whites of eleven eggs beaten to a stiff froth, one and a half cups powdered sugar sifted into the egg, one cup flour, one small teaspoonful cream tartar, same of bitter almonds, little salt; beat the eggs, sugar and flavoring; sift the flour four times, adding the cream tartar the last time; bake from forty to sixty minutes in a slow oven; sift the flour before measuring. The success of this cake depends on its being well beaten. It should be baked in a chimney mould. Turn upside down in a colander to cool, then coax out gently; do not butter the mould.

UNION CAKE.

Four eggs, one cup butter, two cups sugar, four cups flour, one and a half teaspoonfuls cream tartar, one teaspoonful soda in half a cup milk; flavor with nutmeg.

BESSIE'S CAKE.

Two thirds cup butter beaten to a cream, one half cup white sugar, two thirds cup milk, whites of three eggs, one teaspoonful cream tartar, half teaspoonful soda, two heaping cups flour; add milk and flour alternately, lastly whites: flavor with almond.

FRANK'S WASHINGTON PIE.

One scant cup sugar, one half cup butter, two eggs, one fourth cup milk, one and a half cups flour, one teaspoonful cream tartar, one half teaspoonful soda.

MAY L.'S CLOVE CAKE.

One cup sugar, one half cup butter, two cups flour, three fourths cup milk, two eggs, one teaspoonful cream tartar, one half teaspoonful soda, one cup raisins.

VANILLA JUMBLES.

One cup butter, one cup sugar, two eggs, one teaspoonful soda dissolved in two tablespoonfuls sweet milk, two teaspoonfuls cream tartar, two teaspoonfuls vanilla; mix soft and roll.

FILLING FOR WALNUT CAKE.

One cup rolled walnut meats, one cup sweet cream, one half cup sugar; stir in two teaspoonfuls corn starch; let all cook together until thickened, then add meats.

GRANDPA'S CAKE.

Three eggs, two cups sugar, three cups flour, one cup butter, one cup milk, one teaspoonful cream tartar, one half teaspoonful soda, one fourth of a nutmeg grated, pinch salt.

GRACE'S SUGAR COOKIES.

Two eggs, two cups sugar, one cup butter, one teaspoonful soda, six tablespoonfuls sour cream, a little salt if you choose, flavoring.

WHITE CAKE.

Rub half cup butter until creamy, slowly add one cup sugar, then alternately half cup milk and two cups flour in which two teaspoonfuls baking powder have been sifted; flavor with almond or lemon juice; last, fold in the stiffly beaten whites of four eggs; bake in three shallow pans of the same size, and put together with the following.

LEMON FILLING.

Mix a heaping tablespoonful corn starch with one quarter cup cold water, and stir into half cup boiling water; stir till it thickens; add half cup sugar, the beaten yolks of two eggs, and the juice of one large lemon — the grated rind may be used also; one teaspoonful butter may be added. A double boiler, or one saucepan set in another of water should be used. When beginning to cool, spread between the cakes and leave several hours.

FILLING FOR ORANGE CAKE.

Whites of three eggs, juice of one orange, fifteen tablespoonfuls sugar; beat together, spread between layers and outside of cake; pare and pull in pieces two oranges, put on top of cake.

SNAP DOODLE.

One egg, one cup powdered sugar, butter size of a walnut, one cup milk, two cups flour, three teaspoonfuls baking powder; beat very light, pour into a dripping pan; after the cake is done, sift powdered sugar over the top, and over that chocolate or cocoanut; bake twenty minutes in a hot oven; stir the egg, sugar, and butter well together.

NAPOLIANS.

Puff paste cut into pieces about four inches by three, put together with fruit, chocolate, or jelly; frost, and add blanched almonds.

FEATHER CAKE.

One scant cup sugar, one half cup milk, two small tablespoonfuls butter, one egg, one large heaping cup flour, one teaspoonful cream tartar, one half teaspoonful soda.

SILVER CAKE.

Whites of six eggs, two and a half cups sugar, one cup butter, one cup sweet milk, three and a half cups flour, one teaspoonful cream tartar, one half teaspoonful soda, flavor to taste; stir it well.

STELLA'S YELLOW SPONGE CAKE.

One pound sugar, and yolks of ten eggs beat thoroughly; then beat the whites and mix thoroughly with flavoring and a little salt, one half pound flour; stir as little as possible.

EXCELLENT CAKE.

One pound sugar, one half pound butter, one pound flour, one cup milk, six eggs, one teaspoonful soda, two teaspoonfuls cream tartar.

CARRIE'S JELLY CAKE.

Three eggs, one cup sugar, one tablespoonful butter, three tablespoonfuls milk, one coffee cup flour, three teaspoonfuls baking powder.

WHITE CITRON CAKE.

Two cups sugar, half cup butter, whites of four eggs, one cup cold water, three cups sifted flour, two teaspoonfuls baking powder, one and a half teacupfuls sliced citron ; work butter and sugar to a cream, add the water, then two cups flour and one half the egg, which has been beaten to a froth : stir well, then add the rest of the flour, into which has been mixed the baking powder, and lastly the remainder of the egg beaten well ; add citron, and beat again.

COFFEE CAKE.

One cup brown sugar, one cup butter, one cup strained coffee, one cup molasses, three eggs, one pound raisins, two cups flour, two teaspoonfuls baking powder.

LIZZETTE'S WHIST CAKE.

One cup butter, two cups sugar, eight eggs dropped in two at a time, two large spoonfuls milk, two cups flour, one and a half teaspoonfuls cream tartar, one fourth teaspoonful soda ; flavor to taste. Makes two loaves.

BUTTER CAKE.

One cup butter, one cup sugar, four eggs, one cup flour ; flavor with lemon.

CUP CAKE.

Five eggs, one cup butter, two cups sugar, one cup milk, four cups flour, one teaspoonful soda, a little nutmeg, and fruit if you like.

MYRA'S NUT CAKE.

Two thirds cup butter, two cups sugar, beaten ; add yolks three eggs, one cup flour with two teaspoonfuls baking powder, one cup milk, two cups flour, with a large cup nuts ; then add the whites of the eggs beaten to a stiff froth ; frost, cut in squares, and put a half nut on each square.

FIG CAKE.

Two cups sugar, one cup butter, four eggs, one cup milk, three cups flour, one teaspoonful soda, two teaspoonfuls cream tartar, one half pound figs.

COFFEE CAKE.

Two cups brown sugar, one cup molasses, one and a half cups butter, five cups flour, one of strong coffee, four eggs, three tablespoonfuls cinnamon, one tablespoonful cloves, one tablespoonful soda, one pound raisins, one half pound currants.

ARROWHEAD CAKE.

One cup butter, two of sugar, three eggs, one cup sweet milk, three cups flour, three teaspoonfuls baking powder, flavor ; never fails ; good for all kinds of layer cake.

COFFEE CAKE.

Five eggs, two cups sugar, one cup molasses, one full cup butter, one cup cold coffee, five cups flour, one teaspoonful soda ; fruit and spice.

EMMA'S WHITE CAKE.

Two cups sugar, one cup butter, one cup sweet milk, three and a half cups flour, three teaspoonfuls baking powder, whites of eight eggs.

APPLE FILLING FOR LAYER CAKE.

One large or two small apples grated, one lemon grated (rind and juice), one teacupful pulverized sugar; mix together, and set it on the stove five minutes.

PORK CAKE.

One pound salt pork chopped fine; let it boil two minutes in one half pint water; one cup molasses, two cups sugar, three eggs, two teaspoonfuls soda, one pound raisins chopped fine; add nutmeg, cinnamon, and cloves to taste; flour to make a stiff batter.

MRS. C.'S SPONGE CAKE.

Two cups powdered sugar, two cups pastry flour, juice of one lemon, ten eggs; yolks and sugar beaten together; the lemon put in the last thing. Bake one hour.

MRS. T.'S WHITE CAKE.

One and a half cups flour, one cup sugar, one half cup milk, one large tablespoonful butter, whites of three eggs, two teaspoonfuls baking powder; flavor.

EVELYN'S CHOCOLATE CAKE.

One cup sugar, two eggs, one fourth cup butter, one fourth cup milk, one heaping cup flour, one half cup grated chocolate dissolved in one fourth cup boiling water, with one teaspoonful vanilla, one half teaspoonful soda, one teaspoonful cream tartar.

FROSTING.

One cup sugar, one half cup milk, butter size of nutmeg; boil ten minutes, and beat till cold, when it will be like whipped cream. When cold, pour melted chocolate over all; cut in squares and put walnuts on top. Use coffee cups for all measuring.

CREAM CAKE.

Two eggs, one cup sugar, one half cup sweet cream, one and a half cups flour, two teaspoonfuls baking powder.

MRS. W.'S SPONGE CAKE.

Three gills powdered sugar, one half pint pastry flour, five eggs, the juice and grated rind of half a lemon, a little salt; beat the sugar and yolks of the eggs together, then beat the whites to a stiff froth; add the whites, then the flour, lastly the lemon. Bake one half hour in a moderate oven.

ROLL JELLY CAKE.

One cup sugar, three eggs, two teaspoonfuls warm butter, three tablespoonfuls milk, one and a half teaspoonfuls baking powder, one cup flour. Beat eggs, sugar, and butter together; put baking powder into flour and sift, then add the milk. Bake in flat pans; spread with jelly, and roll.

EMMA'S JELLY ROLL.

One cup sugar, four eggs, one cup flour, one half teaspoonful soda, one teaspoonful cream tartar, pinch of salt; bake in a flat pan; spread with jelly, and roll.

FROSTING FOR CAKE.

Beat the whites of one or more eggs to a stiff froth; add five rounding tablespoonfuls powdered sugar for each egg, and beat again. Spread before the cake is entirely cold.

MILK FROSTING.

Boil two cups of sugar and three fourths cup milk nine minutes: whip until cool.

MRS. H.'S CHOCOLATE FROSTING.

For the white of one egg use one half square of Baker's chocolate and four tablespoonfuls sugar. Melt the chocolate over steam, add gradually the sugar, beat the white of the egg to a stiff froth, then beat this into the melted chocolate; flavor with vanilla.

COCOANUT FROSTING.

White of one egg, nine teaspoonfuls sugar; spread on the cake, and strew thickly with cocoanut.

HELEN'S COOKIES.

One and a half cups sugar, one cup butter, two eggs, one teaspoonful cream tartar, one half teaspoonful soda, a little nutmeg, flour to roll.

LEMON SNAPS.

One large cup sugar, two thirds cup butter, half teaspoonful soda dissolved in two teaspoonfuls hot water, flour enough to roll thin; flavor with lemon.

EGG ROCK CAKE.

One cup sugar, four eggs, one cup flour, one teaspoonful soda, two of cream tartar; bake in round tins. Frost both cakes; for the top cake use equal parts of the chocolate frosting and the white filling; for the bottom cake use chocolate frosting. Put the cakes together with the white filling between.

White filling. — White of an egg and one half cup powdered sugar; flavor with pineapple.

CHOCOLATE FROSTING.

One square of Baker's chocolate, the white of one egg, one cup powdered sugar, two tablespoonfuls boiling water; beat two thirds of a cupful of sugar into the unbeaten white of the egg; scrape the chocolate and put it, and the remaining third of a cupful of sugar, and the water, into a small frying pan. Stir over a hot fire until smooth and glossy, and then stir into the beaten white and sugar.

EDNA'S CAKE.

Half a cup butter, one cup sugar, two cups flour, four eggs, one teaspoonful cream tartar, half a teaspoonful soda, dissolved in half a cup milk.

GINGER SNAPS.

One cup butter, one cup each sugar and molasses, boiled together a minute or two; one teaspoonful soda dissolved in a quarter of a cupful of boiling water, flour to roll; flavor with ginger.

MOLLIE'S GINGER SNAPS.

One cup molasses, one half cup butter, boiled a few minutes; add one teaspoonful soda, a little ginger, flour to roll.

MOLASSES CAKE.

Two eggs, one cup molasses, one cup sour cream, one teaspoonful soda, nutmeg, little salt; makes two cakes on round tins.

PLAIN GINGERBREAD.

One cup molasses, one half cup butter, one half cup sweet milk, one egg, one teaspoonful soda, two and a half cups flour.

HARD SUGAR GINGERBREAD.

Two eggs, one and a half cups sugar, one half cup milk, one cup melted butter, two teaspoonfuls ginger, one small teaspoonful soda, flour to roll.

MOLASSES DROP CAKES.

One cup molasses, one half cup sugar, one cup sweet milk, two eggs, butter size of an egg, one teaspoonful soda, with a little ginger and nutmeg.

SOFT GINGERBREAD.

One cup butter, one cup molasses, one cup sugar, one cup sour milk or buttermilk, one teaspoonful soda dissolved in boiling water, one tablespoonful ginger, one teaspoonful cinnamon, two eggs, about five cups flour — enough to make it thick as cup-cake batter, perhaps a trifle thicker — work in four cups first, and add very cautiously. Stir butter, sugar, molasses, and spice together to a light cream ; set them on the range until slightly warm ; beat the eggs light ; add the milk to the warmed mixture, then the eggs, the soda, and lastly the flour. Beat very hard ten minutes, and bake at once in a loaf or in small tins. Half a pound of raisins, seeded and cut in halves, will improve this excellent ginger- bread ; dredge them well before putting them in : add them at the last.

MOLLIE'S COOKIES.

In a coffee cup put one teaspoonful soda, one teaspoon- ful ginger, three tablespoonfuls melted shortening, one table- spoonful boiling water; fill the cup with best New Orleans molasses ; roll about half an inch thick ; two cups will make about fifty cakes.

GINGER SNAPS.

One pint molasses, one cup brown sugar, one table- spoonful soda, one tablespoonful ginger; or, if preferred, make up the tablespoons of equal parts of ginger and cinna- mon ; one cupful shortening — all butter, or half butter and half lard. Directions : Place sugar, molasses, and butter on the stove, and let them come to a boil ; stir spices into the flour, using from four to five cups flour ; dissolve the soda in hot water and pour into the molasses, sugar, and butter, holding it over the flour, as it is very apt to run over; roll very thin.

MRS. L.'S SUGAR COOKIES.

One cup molasses, two thirds cup butter, one half cup sugar, one third cup water, one teaspoonful soda, two teaspoonfuls ginger, flour to roll.

MRS. CRANE'S COOKIES.

One cup butter, one cup molasses, one cup sugar, three fourths cup sweet milk, one teaspoonful soda, two teaspoonfuls ginger, flour to roll.

HATTIE'S COOKIES.

One and a half cups sugar, one cup butter, two eggs, one fourth pound currants, one half teaspoonful soda, one half teaspoonful cinnamon, one half teaspoonful cloves, one half teaspoonful nutmeg.

MOLASSES COOKIES.

One cup molasses, one half cup butter, one half cup sour milk, two teaspoonfuls soda.

DOUGHNUTS No 1.

One cup milk, one cup sugar, one egg, piece of butter size of a small egg, two teaspoonfuls baking powder.

DOUGHNUTS No. 2.

One coffee cup sour milk, two eggs, one cup sugar, one half teaspoonful soda, butter size of an egg, flour enough to roll.

CRULLERS.

Four eggs, four tablespoonfuls melted butter, six tablespoonfuls sugar, four tablespoonfuls sweet milk, one teaspoonful soda, one teaspoonful nutmeg, flour to roll out.

PANCAKES.

One pint sour milk, two thirds cup sugar, three eggs, pinch of salt, a little nutmeg, one tablespoonful melted lard, small teaspoonful soda, flour to make a thick batter; fry in boiling lard.

* PICKLES AND PRESERVES *

"Peter Piper picked a peck of pickled peppers."

PICKLES.

Wash five hundred cucumbers and lay in a tub or crock; sprinkle over them one pint of table salt and cover with boiling water; let them stand twenty-four hours, then drain all the brine from them into a preserving kettle; heat to boiling, and again pour over them; repeat this process three times; after the third heating, wash thoroughly in cold water; line your preserving kettle with clean green cabbage leaves, and put in the cucumbers, adding six green peppers, a stick of horseradish (sliced), and a small bit of alum; then fill the kettle with the best cider vinegar, boiling hot. Let them stand from three to four hours before putting away.

PICKLED PEACHES.

Select ripe peaches and pare them. To one half peck allow three pounds sugar and one pint vinegar. Boil the sugar and vinegar twenty minutes; put the peaches in the boiling liquid and boil until tender. Flavor with stick cinnamon and whole cloves, which should be put into small cloth bags.

CHILI SAUCE.

Twenty-five ripe tomatoes, eleven green peppers, five onions, chop fine; add four cups vinegar, three cups sugar, one tablespoonful salt.

CHOW CHOW.

Chop one peck green tomatoes, six onions, eight green peppers; sprinkle with salt; drain over night; in the morning put in a porcelain kettle with two pounds brown sugar, one tablespoonful each of black pepper, mustard, and celery seed. Cover with vinegar and boil until done.

TOMATO CATCHUP.

Two even tablespoonfuls of salt to one quart of tomatoes; one teaspoonful each of pepper, cloves, allspice, and mace; one tablespoonful mustard, one gill vinegar; boil down one half.

CRANBERRY JELLY.

One quart of cranberries, one pint of water, one pint of sugar; boil thirty minutes, then strain into a mould.

CRANBERRY SAUCE.

Take one quart of water and one pint of sugar; put over the fire and boil five or ten minutes; then put in the berries and let them simmer about twenty minutes without stirring; pour out, and the berries will be nearly all whole and transparent.

SPICED CURRANTS.

Five pounds of currants, four pounds of sugar, one pint of vinegar, two tablespoonfuls of cassia, two of cloves. Boil two hours.

PRESERVED STRAWBERRIES.

To one pound of berries use three fourths of a pound of sugar in layers. Place in kettle on back of the stove until the sugar is dissolved into syrup; then let come to a boil, stirring from the bottom; spread on platters, not too thickly, and set it out in the hot sun till the syrup thickens — it may take two or three days; keep in tumblers like jelly. Strawberries done in this way retain their color and flavor.

FOODS AND DRINKS FOR THE SICK.

"Now good digestion waits on appetite, and health on both."
—Shakespeare.

BEEF TEA.

Fill a glass can with lean beef cut in small pieces; cover closely, and set in a kettle of cold water. Boil until the juice is all extracted.

CHICKEN BROTH.

Boil the first and second joints of a chicken in one quart of water until tender; season with a very little salt and pepper.

TAPIOCA PUDDING.

An even tablespoonful of tapioca soaked for two hours in nearly a cup of new milk; stir into this the yolk of a fresh egg, a little sugar, a little salt, and bake it in a cup fifteen minutes.

RICE.

Fresh boiled rice, wet with the juice of roast beef or mutton, and served on a piece of toast, is nice.

JELLY WATER.

One large teaspoonful currant jelly, one goblet ice-water, beaten well together.

EGG NOG.

Beat a perfectly fresh egg with an egg beater; then add two teaspoonfuls wine, two teaspoonfuls cream, two small teaspoonfuls sugar, a little nutmeg.

EGG NOG.

One egg — the yolk beaten first, then the white ; add two teaspoonfuls of sugar and beat again ; then the juice of half a lemon and the juice of one orange.

DELICIOUS.

The white of one egg beaten to a stiff froth, sweeten to taste ; add the juice of half a lemon.

MILK PUNCH. (D. C.)

One tumbler milk well sweetened, two tablespoonfuls best brandy well stirred in. Give very cold with ice.

SAGO CREAM.

Take a dessert spoonful of sago and boil in clear water until reduced to a jelly : add a cup of sweet cream, boil again ; beat up a fresh egg very light, pour the sago on it while hot ; sweeten, and spice to taste.

BAKED MILK.

Bake two quarts of milk eight or ten hours in a moderate oven, in a jar covered with writing paper tied down. It will be thick like cream. Good for very weak persons.

CARRIE'S ORANGE CREAM.

The juice of six oranges, one fourth of a pound of white sugar, one pint of boiling water, and six eggs. Beat the yolks, add sugar, orange juice, and water, and stir over boiling water until it thickens. When cool put into glasses, and on each one put the beaten whites, sweetened and flavored with a little of the grated rind.

FLAXSEED TEA.

Put to two tablespoonfuls whole flaxseed a pint of boiling water, and boil fifteen minutes; cut up one lemon and put in a pitcher with two tablespoonfuls of sugar. Strain the tea boiling hot into the pitcher and stir together.

CODFISH SOUP.

Freshen a little codfish in cold water; pour this off and add hot water, crackers, and butter or cream.

WINE JELLY.

One half box gelatine, one cup cold water, let it stand; one pint boiling water, one and a half lemons, one cup sugar, one pint wine; strain into moulds.

❋ CONFECTIONERY ❋

"Sweets to the sweet."

WALNUT CREAMS.

Break into a dish the white of an egg; add the same quantity of water, and stir stiff with confectioner's sugar. Roll a portion of the cream thick, cut into round pieces; lay an English walnut meat on each piece, or place the cream between two meats.

WALNUT CHOCOLATE CREAMS.

Lay English walnut meats between two round pieces of cream; mould into shape with the fingers, and when hard dip in melted chocolate.

PEPPERMINTS.

Two cups sugar, one half cup water, boil five minutes; flavor to taste with peppermint; stir until thick, and drop on white paper.

WALNUTS

Must be cracked so that the halves remain perfect, and shaken well in a cloth to rid them of dust.

ICE CREAM CANDY.

Two cups sugar, one half cup water, one fourth teaspoonful cream tartar; boil ten minutes without stirring; when nearly done add piece of butter size of an English walnut; pull it as hot as possible, and while pulling put flavoring on your hands.

MOLASSES CANDY.

One pint molasses, one cup brown sugar, one fourth cup butter; boil until brittle; try it by dropping into cold water; pour in buttered plates to cool, and begin to pull as soon as cool enough to handle. For chocolate caramels, add two squares Baker's chocolate to the above, and do not boil quite as long.

TOP.

One square chocolate, one cup pulverized sugar. Soften with two tablespoonfuls milk and two tablespoonfuls water; let it boil three or five minutes.

NUT CARAMEL.

Four cups granulated sugar, three tablespoonfuls glucose, one cup water; boil, stirring frequently, until it will harden when dropped in cold water; add immediately one cup cream or one half cup rich milk, and a small piece of butter; boil again until it hardens in water; remove from the stove and flavor with two teaspoonfuls of vanilla; add two cups of walnut meats; pour into a buttered pan, and when nearly cold cut up in square blocks.

FIG CANDY.

One cup sugar, one third cup water, one fourth teaspoonful cream tartar; do not stir while boiling; boil to an amber color; stir in the cream tartar just before taking from the fire; wash the figs, open and lay in a tin pan, and pour the candy over them.

MOLASSES CANDY.

One cup molasses, one cup sugar, one tablespoonful vinegar, piece of butter, one half teaspoonful soda; add soda as you take it from the fire; this cooks in a short time.

HINTS TO HOUSEKEEPERS.

"Many things impossible to thought
Have been by need to full perfection brought."

SALT eaten with nuts aids digestion.

THE surest way to have clear jelly is to let the juice drain through a flannel bag without squeezing it.

KEEP a little beeswax tied up in a cloth to rub your flatirons with.

MILDEW. — Rub the spot with soft soap and salt, and expose to the sun.

CURE FOR HOARSENESS. — Bake a lemon for twenty minutes in the oven; open at one end and take out the inside; thicken it with sugar and eat.

LEMON MOSS. — Put a few sprigs of moss to soak, after being washed, in water enough to make a drink the thickness of cream; after standing a short time, add lemon juice and loaf sugar. Good for a cold on the lungs.

EGG NOG. — Yolks of six eggs, six tablespoonfuls of powdered sugar, one quart new milk, one half pint French brandy, a little nutmeg; beat the whites separately, and stir through the mixture just before you serve.

❊ MISCELLANEOUS ❊

SURE CURE FOR CARPET BUGS. — Equal parts of nitrate potash, pulverized camphor gum, and pulverized borax mixed together.

To WASH doubtful calicoes, dissolve one teaspoonful sugar of lead in one pailful water, and soak the garment fifteen minutes before washing.

MILDEW. — Dip the stained cloth in buttermilk, and lay in the sun.

To CLEAN STRAW MATTING. — Wash with a cloth dipped in clean salt and water; then wipe dry at once. This prevents it from turning yellow.

COAL FIRE. — If the coal fire is low, throw on a tablespoonful of salt, and it will brighten it very much.

To CLEANSE A SPONGE. — By rubbing a fresh lemon thoroughly into a soured sponge and rinsing it several times in lukewarm water, it will become as sweet as when new.

A FLANNEL cloth dipped into warm soap suds, then into whiting and applied to paint, will remove all dirt and grease. Wash with clean water and dry. The most delicate paint will not be injured, and will look like new.

To REMOVE paint splashed upon window panes, use a hot solution of soda, and rub with a soft flannel.

A REMEDY for chapped hands is to rub them in vinegar after washing, and let them dry without wiping. It will keep the hands soft and white.

TABLE OF WEIGHTS AND MEASURES.

Two cups of sifted flour is equal to one pound.
One pint of sifted flour is equal to one pound.
One pint of packed butter is equal to one pound.
Ten eggs are equal to one pound.
Two cupfuls are equal to one pint.
Two wineglassfuls are equal to one gill.

WHAT A WOMAN SHOULD WEIGH.

A WOMAN whose height is

5 feet, 0 inches, should weigh 118 pounds.
5 feet, 1 inch, should weigh 124 pounds.
5 feet, 2 inches, should weigh 128 pounds.
5 feet, 3 inches, should weigh 130 pounds.
5 feet, 4 inches, should weigh 136 pounds.
5 feet, 5 inches, should weigh 139 pounds.
5 feet, 6 inches, should weigh 143 pounds.
5 feet, 7 inches, should weigh 148 pounds.
5 feet, 8 inches, should weigh 153 pounds.
5 feet, 9 inches, should weigh 153 pounds.

This table is for women between twenty and forty-five years of age. After that they become heavier. A woman should weigh but little less than a man in proportion to her height. The bust of a perfectly formed woman should measure ten inches more than her waist.

WHETHER present or absent, alone or in company, speak up for one another, earnestly and lovingly.

OFTEN, after cooking a meal, a person will feel tired and have no appetite. For this beat a raw egg until light; stir in a little milk, sugar, and nutmeg; drink half an hour before eating.

FOR a cold on the chest, a flannel rag wrung out in boiling water and sprinkled with turpentine, laid on the chest, gives the greatest relief.

TO STOP bleeding, bind a handful of flour on the cut.

IF the saucepan in which milk is to be boiled be first moistened with water, it will prevent the milk from burning.

INDEX.